The Heart of
AUSTRALIA

PHOTOGRAPHY AND TEXT BY
PETER JARVER

THUNDERHEAD PUBLISHING
Darwin Australia

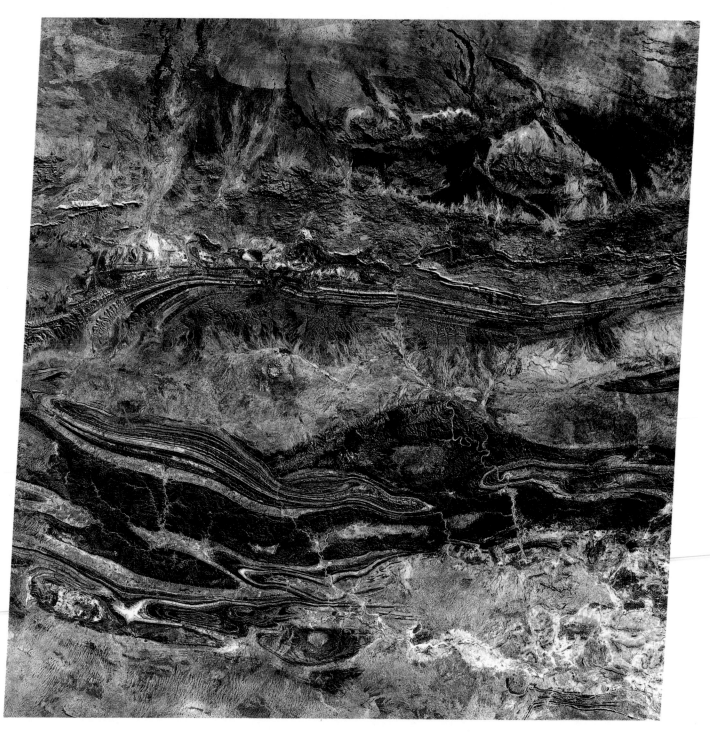

Landsat image of the western Macdonnell Range area taken from a height of 920 kilometres.

CONTENTS

FOREWORD

The vast flat landscape of the Australian Continent is perhaps how all the continents will look when they are as old and worn as The Great South Land. For a thousand million years the wind and rains have eroded away enormous mountain ranges, and the periodic cycling of Ice Ages has alternately locked in ice or nourished tropical conditions in this large island known as Australia. Mankind has been interacting with the landscape for only a small fraction of this time, and his ability to effect changes to the environment on any sizable scale has been possible for only the last couple of hundred years — a mere blink of the eye in the overall life of our planet. But with the advent of machines our ability to alter or destroy large areas (or develop, as some wealthy and powerful persons pretend), has increased out of all proportion to our physical size and strength. Rainforests are disappearing at a mind-numbing rate of 40 hectares per minute. That is every hour of every day of the year. Coastal resort development is the optimistic view of marine environment destruction. The breeding grounds of our prawns and fish are under immense threat from the large number or building proposals right on the foreshore. The mangrove areas where breeding takes place are considered to be mosquito infested swamps, suitable only for landfill and building upon.

With the advent of a more global outlook and the problems associated with severe pollution and unrestrained clearing of vast tracts of land, there is a growing realization that our planet is running out of time. Our air and water are becoming increasingly poisoned, our soils suffer from salination and erosion. Indeed, we are threatening our very existence by our short-sighted outlook and concern for short term material gain. However, during our brief stay on this one and only planet we have, our role is that of guardian and keeper for future generations, not of plunderer and despoiler for our self-indulgent use. We are after all, responsible for what we hand down to our children.

On a planetary basis Australia is the most fortunate of the continents. For at least 40,000 years this vast landscape was populated by Aboriginal people on a small scale only. They lived in harmony with the land, and through a complex social and spiritual system looked after the earth which nourished them, taking only what they needed, when it was required. The use of fire for hunting purposes was the only means by which the landscape was altered and while there are indications that this technique changed the ecology of Australia upon their arrival, their harmonious lifestyle has kept a balance over the ensuing millenia.

The arrival of European people on our shores 200 years ago has left an indelible mark in a very short time. We have built large cities along the coastline and cleared much of the original tree cover, causing large scale disruptions and numerous extinctions of the original flora and fauna. Successive governments have rushed headlong into enticing ever more people onto our largely arid continent using the catchcry of "populate or perish", with the result of placing ever-increasing pressure on our natural resources. To help pay for our indulgent and wasteful lifestyles, governments in their myopic wisdom allow the sale of our most wondrous natural assets — the tall forests of the southern regions, some of which contain the largest flowering trees on earth. In return for their cheap sale we are sent paper and cardboard boxes containing the objects of our material desires.

Fortunately for our embattled land, the major population centres have con-

fined themselves to the coastal regions. For such a modest number of people, Australia is one of the most urbanized countries in the world. This has meant that relatively little pressure has been placed on the vast interior, if for no other reason than the harshness of the climate and the enormous distances involved have defeated all but the most recent technological advances. Apart from a few mining ventures, the only other activity to encroach on this enormous area is the cattle industry, and although it has undoubtedly had some impact on the land, this is not always apparent.

For the heart of Australia then, the impact has been minimal. Much of the country would look the same as before Europeans came. Vast tracts of mulga bush, majestic desert oaks and ghost gums, along with the countless spinifex balls which meld into golden fields in the distance, live in a landscape virtually unchanged. The air here is not polluted. In fact the sky has such a depth of blue it seems unnatural. On calm days when clear skies allow the smallest detail on any horizon to be discerned, it seems that there is no air at all. Of the little surface water around, most is in the gorges and river beds of the various ranges which give the Centre its unique character. Many of these scenic gorges are located within parks or reserves and so are protected from intrusion by feral animals. As the soils are rarely used for agricultural purposes, there is little use of the various chemicals for fertilizing and pest control.

Perhaps the main threat comes from the several feral animals which have been introduced but not controlled. The camels, donkeys and horses which were used in years gone by for the transportation of supplies, and then with the best of intentions, released into the wild when motorized transport became available, have multiplied into significant populations. These large animals, along with periodic rabbit plagues, compete with native animals for the restricted food sources available. Measures are now being taken to control these threats.

The one other threat to the area are people themselves. A proliferation of four wheel drive vehicles allows easy access to even the remotest of places. Central Australia has a beauty all of its own, which, in combination with the low population and large tracts of unspoilt wilderness, attracts many Australians as well as overseas visitors to experience the solitude and peace of camping out under the stars. A few of the major gorges are accessible only after a considerable drive, but more and more often the fast lane of bitumen highway allows quick and easy passage to the different areas of interest. Proposals are being made to bring together the many small and separate parks under the umbrella of a Macdonnell Range National Park. This would allow better management of both people and feral animals and help preserve the magnificent gorges found within the stunningly picturesque Macdonnell Ranges.

To many people, Central Australia embodies the very image of our great outback, with Ayers Rock symbolizing the grandeur and presence which this ancient landscape holds. While the rest of our continent and indeed the planet is under increasing threat, the heart of Australia remains an island of hope. The inspiration and inner peace which can be gained from a wilderness experience will be available to all future generations if we give thought and action now towards the preservation of our heritage.

Peter Jarver

CENTRAL AUSTRALIA MAP

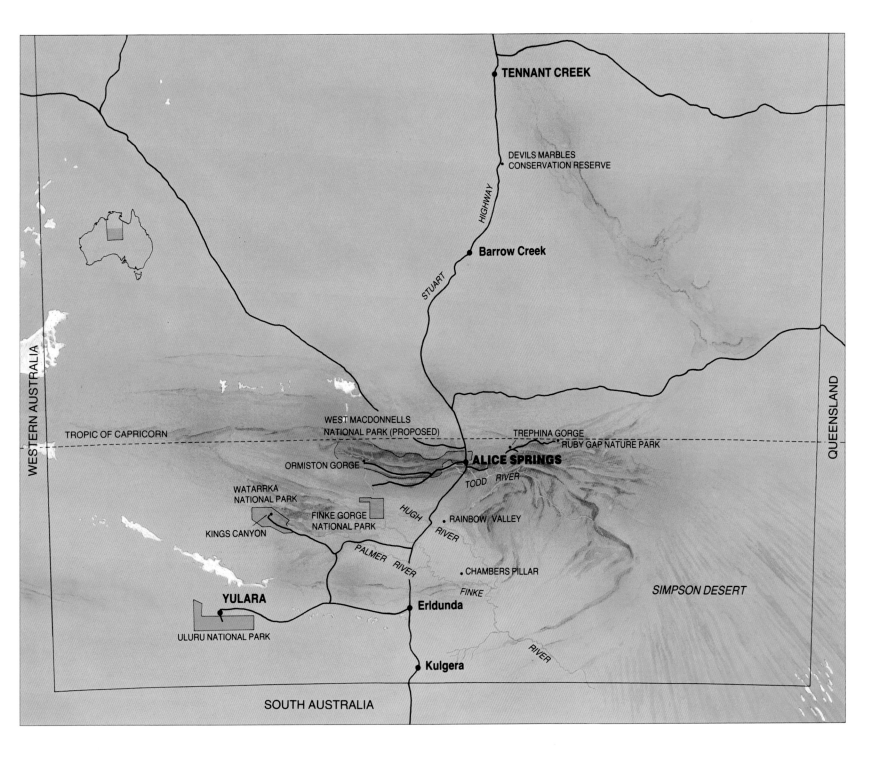

Macdonnell

RANGES

THE MACDONNELL RANGES

The most striking view of the Macdonnell Ranges can be had from one of the tall peaks which are scattered along its 400 kilometre length, or perhaps from an aircraft flying at an even greater altitude. From these perspectives, the long parallel lines of hills which make up the structure of these ancient mountains becomes very apparent. On a clear day, the line of peaks marching across the landscape disappears behind the curvature of the earth. On a hazy day, when trade winds whip up dust from the extensive sandy deserts to the south, the numerous folds and clefts become noticeable, together with the prominent parallel nature of the several ridges which comprise these intriguing ranges.

Situated in the heart of Australia, the Macdonnells are responsible for the very unique nature of this arid part of our continent. A land of red rocky ridges, white-sanded river beds and the haunting ghost gum, Central Australia is to many people the very essence of our vast outback.

The ranges rise steeply from the surrounding plains, exposing themselves as layer upon layer of uplifted and twisted stone, weathered and eroded into imposing shapes and deeply cut gorges. It is here at the cool shady gorges that a startling realization occurs. The larger rivers which flow out of the Macdonnells do not just follow the valleys lying between the parallel ridges, they actually cut through the ranges, directly across the grain of the country. This is quite remarkable when one considers the hard quartzite rock which comprises much of these ranges; however this apparent paradox may be explained by looking back into geological history.

Ancient mountain ranges, believed to have risen to some 5,000 metres in height once covered this area. With the passage of time and the process of erosion, deep layers of sediment were deposited and compressed into the hard quartzite rock we know today. Two thousand million years ago however, these layers were all horizontal.

The Alice Springs Orogeny, a period of major mountain building, began some 350 million years ago. It caused the marked folding and faulting of these layers, some of which are so steeply tilted they are vertical. The various other ranges of the centre such as the George Gill Range, the Krichauff Range and the Waterhouse Range, all of which run parallel to the Macdonnell Ranges, were formed during this same period.

So at a time when all the mountains were considerably higher than at present, the location of the major watercourses were probably fixed in approximately their current positions. Over the long period since then, erosion has taken several thousand metres of rock from the Alice Springs area, the rivers transporting many of the fragments away, and at the same time continuing to cut down across the major ridges. Taking advantage of any natural weaknesses, such as faulting, jointing or intrusion of softer materials, the rivers which were once flowing across a higher land surface have continued to cut down at these points, creating the magnificent gaps and gorges we know today.

The most impressive gorges are in the West Macdonnells, divided from their eastern extension by the town of Alice Springs. These cool, shaded, rock-walled watercourses offer a haven from the sun-scorched plains beyond. Several, such as Ormiston, Glen Helen and Ellery have permanent waterholes, while most of the others, although they frequently do have water, are subject to drying out over prolonged periods of drought.

Since nearly all of the gorges have a north-south aspect, they receive the hot summer sun for only part of the day. As the sun lowers for the afternoon, one wall will become shaded, but will be illuminated by light bouncing off the other.

The soft light reflecting into the shaded side of the gorge warms up the already orange and red coloured stone even further, occasionally seeming to set the gorge on fire. There is an ethereal glow to this soft filtered light.

Many of the gorges are home to an array of plants which are not found beyond their protective red rock walls. The Macdonnell Ranges cycad is as ancient as the mountains themselves and has survived from a wetter time when dinosaurs walked the earth. Slow growing, most of the cycads currently there began as seedlings over a century ago. Perhaps even more amazing is the survival of the red cabbage palm, found only in Palm Valley and the Finke River. Isolated from any other palms by nearly 1,000 kilometres of arid country, these magnificent tall palms crowd together in dense stands and are a relic of a climate which was once much wetter. They are found nowhere else in the world.

The many waterholes found in the various gorges sustain a wide variety of bird and animal life, although the nocturnal habits of many mean they are only seen in the early morning or late afternoon. Euros and rock wallabies are common along the rock areas that are found throughout the ranges and are the largest of the animals. Bird life is indeed prolific, and varies from the enormous wedge-tailed eagle down to the tiny finches which huddle together in large chirping flocks. But perhaps the most surprising visitors are the several water birds which move around the larger waterholes. Apart from herons, ducks and cormorants, occasional appearances are even made by pelicans and swans. Their presence can only be supported if there are fish, and perhaps the most unexpected inhabitants of this arid area are the ten native fish species which may be found in the six permanent waterholes of the Western Macdonnells. In times of good rainfall, they breed very quickly and can soon be found long distances downstream, but as most of the temporary waterholes are short-lived in this climate of sporadic rainfall, their existence is somewhat uncertain.

The inherent beauty of these enticing gorges is further enhanced by the amazing white ghost gum. Looking serenely cool on the hottest of days, they stand in stark contrast to the warm colours of the craggy ledges, seemingly defying any logic as to where a tree should grow.

While the gaps and gorges are the focal points of the Macdonnells and offer scenic grandeur which is unique to the heart of Australia, the imposing peaks of this rugged range impart their own challenge. Devoid of surface water, the arduous climb in the fierce heat of summer would not make for inspired bushwalking. Viewed however from the valleys between the parallel ridges, each prominent peak takes on its own character. Mount Liebig and Mount Zeil both top 1,500 metres but, while only a little lower at 1,334 metres, Mount Sonder is the best known and most impressive. Seen easily from near Glen Helen Gorge, the colour and character of this rock monolith changes continuously as the sun traverses the sky.

Although the Macdonnell Ranges are not particularly high as far as mountains go, the incredibly long period of weathering and shaping has created a unique set of parallel ridges which together form the imposing peaks and escarpments that jut out abruptly from the vast desert areas to the south. Add to this the wonderful gorges with their life-giving waterholes and cool, shady aspects and you have an area of unforgettable beauty which calls you back again and again.

An aerial view of the western Macdonnell Ranges, showing the long east-west ridges which dominate the landscape.

Steeply tilted layers of rock bisect the view from Emily Gap towards Alice Springs.

The distinctive ridge of the eastern Macdonnell Ranges is dominated by Mount Undoolya.

Scattered ghost gums contrast vividly with an approaching thunderstorm, which is about to deluge the prom

of the Macdonnell Ranges. This landscape was made famous by the Aboriginal painter Albert Namatjira.

Silver indigo bushes crowd the foreground, with the distant view of the Macdonnells limited by a heavy shower.

Spinifex clad ridges of the Macdonnell Ranges define one side of a valley which stretches from Alice Springs to beyond Glen Helen.

A small group of ducks make Trephina Gorge home, after good rainfall has filled the main waterhole.

The Hale River continues to carve the magnificent Ruby Gorge. Pink garnet sands gave the false impression to early prospectors that rubies were to be found in abundance.

A small creek divides around a twisted river red gum during its once-a-year flow.

Stately river red gums lean in random directions along the creekbed of Standley Chasm.

The morning sun highlights the delicate featherhead flower, growing on the lower slopes at the western end of the Macdonnell Ranges.

Pink mulla mulla flowers grow in crowded profusion after heavy autumn rains.

Spinifex clad hills fold into a valley to reveal Mount Sonder in the distance.

The steep western slopes of Ormiston Pound conceal the entrance to Ormiston Gorge.

Simpsons Gap shows the tapering formation which typifies the numerous gaps and gorge entrances of the Macdonnell Ranges.

The steep upward thrust of these quartzite ridges continues to defy the erosion process which has given much of the
Macdonnell Ranges its more gentle character.

Vertical layers of sandstone, known as the Organ Pipes, continue their defiant thrust on the banks of the Finke River at Glen Helen.

The imposing sheer-walled cliffs of Standley Chasm allow a narrow view onto rugged quartzite ridges.

The narrow cleft of Redbank Gorge has vertical walls of polished rock. Sand deposited by the 1988 flood allowed walking for the first time, but has since been washed away.

A pair of ghost gums grow in a seemingly impossible position on the rock wall of a wind-swept gorge.

The stark white trunk of a magnificent ghost gum contrasts vividly with the deep blue skies of Central Australia.

A line of mulga bushes encircle an area of ruby dock, a flower commonly found in Central Australia after abundant rains.

A prominent quartzite ridge of the eastern Macdonnell Range overlooks the lower hills and plains of an arid landscape.

Mulga bushes extend across the plains to the distant peaks of Harts Range, a rugged area just to the north of the Macdonnells.

The sheer northern rock face of Ormiston Gorge dominates the rock-strewn creekbed below.

Tranquil stretches of Ormiston Creek provide one of the few fish breeding habitats in Central Australia.

The colours of the late afternoon sun are reflected off the smooth waters of Cycad Gorge in Palm Valley.

The wind-swept surface of a small waterhole still reflects the late afternoon glow from the high walls of Ruby Gorge.

A cluster of the Macdonnell Ranges cycads continues to defy the occasional torrents of floodwaters which flow through Serpentine Gorge at infrequent intervals.

A well-defined spinifex ring near the entrance to Palm Valley.

Isolated spinifex bushes meld into thicker clumps near the base of Mount Sonder.

Morning light reveals the imposing beauty of Mount Sonder, which at 1,400 metres is one of the higher peaks of the western Macdonnells.

Steeply inclined layers of rock thrust out of the plains surrounding Jessie Gap. The watercourse has only just stopped flowing.

The magnificent red cabbage palm in Finke Gorge National Park forms relic stands which are found nowhere else in the world, and which have survived here for thousands of years as the rest of the area has become increasingly arid.

The flowing vertical ridges of the Organ Pipes terminate abruptly at the edge of the Finke River, where powerful flows of water have pushed their way through.

The view along the Finke River, north from Glen Helen, shows clean, sandy waterholes flanked by thick stands of bullrush.

Dense stands of spinifex define the lower slopes of the eastern Macdonnells.

Folded ridges of rock are layered with lines of spinifex, creating interesting visual patterns.

Southern DESERTS

SOUTHERN DESERTS

To many people the idea of a desert brings to mind endless rolling sand dunes with no vegetation and no life. While such deserts do exist, they are not found in Australia, and despite the fact that nearly half the landmass of our continent is classed as desert, there is a great diversity of plants and animals which have adapted superbly to the arid conditions that prevail.

Defined as areas with less than 250 millimetres of rainfall in a year, the two major deserts in the heart of Australia, the Western Desert and Arunta Desert, are usually sub-divided into smaller areas which represent the varying nature of this vast inland plain. One of these, the Simpson Desert, sweeps into the south-east corner of the Northern Territory, bringing with it long lines of sand dunes spaced from 100 metres to a kilometre apart on a flat plain, looking for all the world like enormous rolling waves on a smooth sea.

As one moves westward, the long organised dunes of the Simpson are disrupted into scattered regions of randomly orientated dunes by the hills and ranges of the Alice Springs area. Where the lines of numerous ranges begin to disappear to the east, and the frequency of sandhills increases, the vast expanse of the Western Desert begins once again to dominate the landscape.

The power of the desert is its stark simplicity, uncluttered by horizon-masking trees and lacking the distraction of shady gorges and riverbeds. There is little visual variation in the dominant forms of sky, sand and stunted shrubs providing the total environment. With the approach of evening, the very last rays of the sun set fire to the crests of the highest dunes. As soon as the large shimmering globe has disappeared below the horizon, the sky above the opposite horizon displays the sweeping pink band which defines the earth's shadow through its own atmosphere. This is the shadow of night, so easily seen in the empty stillness of the twilight. Moving across the sky with surprising haste, this pink twilight zone draws after it the lonely grey of the approaching night and the first twinkle of the brightest stars. With the failing light and darkening sky comes an increasing awareness of the vastness of the night, accentuated by the number of stars. In total darkness the profusion of stars is compelling, and one's focus is drawn to the bright swathe of our own Milky Way. With the realization that there are more stars than there are grains of sand on every beach and desert on earth, one momentarily feels alone and insignificant. But then one realizes that if there are that many stars then surely there must be countless planets out there with people just like us wondering about the stars they see.

The flash of a meteorite trail brings you back to the reality of the desert, with its freezing winter nights and searing summer days, and long periods of drought punctuated by heavy flood rains. The desert is a land of extremes. The seemingly lifeless dunes are in fact a haven for the many small creatures and plants that have adapted to the wide variations in the weather. While during the day the wind smooths out the dunes surface into sandy ripples, the early morning reveals a maze of criss-crossing tracks, evidence of the heavy traffic from the night before. Nocturnal habits are common here amongst the wildlife, as moisture must be conserved during the fierce heat of the day. Most active are the various birds, who are able to utilize the updraughts of air as the wind is pushed up the face of the sand dunes.

The few hardy plants that can endure the long periods without rain support the numerous insects, and form the basis of the desert ecosystem. When the rains do come, an explosion of growth takes place. Bushes and lone trees begin an immediate growth cycle, perhaps the first in several years, but the most noticeable effect is the multitude of wildflowers which burst forth from the myriad seeds hidden beneath the sandy desert floor. They appear in such vast numbers in places that the ground is literally carpeted in flowers. The colours are intense as each individual plant competes for the attention of the many insects that help to continue the growth cycles.

While the deserts cover large tracts to the south of the Macdonnell Ranges, the generally flat area is punctuated by some stunning and mysterious geological formations. Most famous of these are Ayers Rock and the Olgas. Jutting out from the sandy soil these monoliths are awesome in their size, and impose a compelling presence on all who are drawn to their remote location. Just as mysterious is Chambers Pillar, an isolated rock column on the edge of the Simpson Desert. Rising abruptly from a small rocky mound, the soft sandstone column thrusts about 35 metres above the surrounding plain. This prominent outcrop was first sighted by John McDouall Stuart in 1860, and for many years it was used as a reference point for the hardy travellers game enough to venture into this area.

The cliffs of Rainbow Valley provide a spectacular display as the last rays of sunset fire up the deep red colour which caps this free standing bluff. Forming part of the edge of the James Range, this major feature became isolated from the main range eons ago, and is now situated beside a large barren claypan. The stark emptiness of the scene creates the impression of a lunar landscape.

At the western end of the George Gill Range, where the vast sands of the southern deserts meet the first of the many ranges, lies perhaps the most spectacular of all the gorges in the heart of Australia, Kings Canyon. Situated in Watarrka National Park, the area is very important botanically, as it contains plant species from both the deserts and the Macdonnell Range area, including several rare and relict species. But it is the imposing scenery and diversity of landscape that makes Kings Canyon so special. The gorge itself begins as a wide unassuming entrance, and tapers into a narrow sheer-sided canyon which follows a boulder strewn watercourse, at the head of which the two walls meet in a large curving rock face. In times of heavy rain, water plunges over a gap in this wall, forming Central Australia's most impressive waterfall. Above the boulders and cycads of the canyon itself, lies the Garden of Eden, a lush cycad-fringed series of waterholes which form another gorge at right angles to the canyon. The plateau surrounding those gorges consists of a maze of weathered sandstone domes, any one of which looks very similar to the many others. Known as the Lost City, one could easily become disorientated in this labyrinth of rock domes.

Deserts are the keepers of many secrets, with the shifting sands covering tomorrow what is here today. The sands of the Simpson Desert are not the remains of the ancestral mountains of the present-day Macdonnell Ranges, but have been blown northward from the Lake Eyre region by the persistent south-easterly winds. Beginning some five million years ago, the vast dunefields have been organized into parallel lines up to 300 kilometres in length, only occasionally converging. Viewed from the great altitude of a commercial airliner, these long lines of reddish sand extend from one horizon to the other, an enormous sea of sand. However the deserts have not always been so arid. In times gone by the climate was much wetter, with a greater diversity of plants and animals. Only 20,000 years ago did the area begin to dry out and so create this arid region. The sands will go on shifting long after we are gone, but for as long as people continue to live in the heart of Australia, some will be drawn to the quiet sands of the desert, in order to experience the solitude it offers.

Stars trail through the night sky, as the moon illuminates a large dune in the Simpson Desert.

Tangled mulla mulla and burr daisies cover the side of a sand dune.

The imposing line of a sand dune marches off towards the horizon, leaving below the flat barren landscape of the Simpson Desert.

Glowing warmly in the setting sun, Chambers Pillar is a prominent landmark dominating the surrounding plain.

Long spiky leaves of a grass tree clump spray out proudly beneath two large flower stalks.

Late season wildflowers cover the sandy soil around the base of an isolated outcrop near the Ooraminna Range.

Wildflowers partially cover one of the several low sand dunes which are scattered around the base of Chambers Pillar.

The moonlike landscape of Rainbow

with a fiery intensity from the setting sun.

The rising moon and light from a campfire add a warm glow to this outcrop of Train Hills.

The sheer southern wall of Kings Canyon makes an imposing sight when viewed from the top of the gorge.

Recent geological movements have shaped the smooth northern wall of Kings Canyon.

The soft glow of twilight illuminates the tree-lined creek leading into the main gorge of Kings Canyon.

A lush grove of cycads lines the permanent waterhole above Kings Canyon known as the Garden of Eden.

Where the long walls of the canyon meet, cycads crowd around the splashpool of a rarely flowing waterfall.

Numerous domes of weathered sandstone create an alien landscape above Kings Canyon.

Clean white bushes of tangled mulla mulla contrast vividly with the red sand of an elevated dune on the edge of the Simpson Desert.

A dazzling carpet of wildflowers is a relatively common sight after monsoonal rains soak a parched landscape.

Near Andado, rare Acacia Peuce trees form a tiny forest within the enormous surrounds of the Simpson Desert.

Around About

THE ALICE

AROUND ABOUT THE ALICE

It is ironic that the ranges surrounding Alice Springs, which stand in the centre of a vast continent several thousand kilometres from the oceans that encircle Australia, had their beginnings in the seas that once covered this area. The inland sea has long since vanished, and the surrounding country has become an arid area with a unique beauty all of its own. While Aboriginal people have lived on this land for tens of thousands of years, Alice Springs, the lifeline of this remote area of European settlement, was surveyed as a town in only 1888.

At this time it was known as Stuart, named after John McDouall Stuart, who in 1860 was the first white person to pass through the area. In fact Stuart's journey took him through a gap in the Macdonnell Ranges created by the Hugh River, some 40 kilometres to the west of Alice Springs, and it was not until surveyors of the Overland Telegraph arrived in 1871 that Heavitree Gap was first sighted. It was decided that this natural break in the ranges would be ideal for the new transcontinental line to pass through on its way further north to Darwin, from which point Australia was connected to the rest of the world. The task of installing the overland Telegraph was mammoth. From Adelaide the single wire communications line had to travel some 3,500 kilometres through the heart of Australia, across country which was still largely unknown. The job was completed in two years and is a tribute to the hardy souls who worked in such harsh conditions. Repeater stations were needed to maintain the strength of the signal, and since water was found in the Todd River, one of the nine repeater stations was built at Alice spring, situated several kilometres north of Heavitree Gap.

The presence of this relay station focussed attention on the largely unexplored areas surrounding this tiny outpost of civilization, and in due course the discovery of alluvial gold toward the east at Arltunga placed a new importance on the station as a supply base. In addition, a fledgling pastoral industry was beginning to develop, supplying meat to the telegraph operators, linesmen and miners. When the railway from the south reached Oodnadatta in 1889, transport became available to ship the cattle to southern markets.

For many years then, Stuart was the administrative centre for the increasing mining activities in the Centre along with the associated businesses of transport and supplies. The population increased very slowly, such that by 1927 only 40 people lived there, of which 12 were children. The decision had been made to extend the railway from Oodnadatta to Stuart, and work commenced in January 1927. Two years later the first train arrived from Adelaide, and, as a consequence of greatly lowered transport costs and faster, more reliable connections, the white population began to grow. In 1933, when the name of the town was officially changed to Alice Springs, the population had swelled to over 500.

During the Second World War Alice Springs became an important staging post because it was here that troops and supplies had to be off-loaded from the railway, and re-organised for road transportation further north to Darwin. In a short space of time more than 3,000 military personnel were stationed here, and with the bombing of Darwin by the Japanese in 1942, Alice Springs temporarily became the administrative centre for the Northern Territory.

After the war prosperous times returned, with the character and shape of the Alice we know today emerging in the '50s and '60s. With a current population of around 23,000 Alice Springs looks like any other modern town except that it is situated in an arid area. The railway still finishes here, despite the numerous attempts to have it extended to Darwin. The pastoral industry is still strong, mining has a presence but not to the extent that it once did, while tourism is now the other major employer. The beautiful gorges of the Macdonnell Ranges have a unique beauty which draws people from all around the world.

The view from atop Anzac Hill in the centre of Alice Springs reveals the imposing Macdonnell Ranges to the south, where the long line running east-west terminates unexpectedly at Heavitree Gap. It is here that the Todd River passes through the ranges on its course out into the Simpson Desert. A river by shape and form, it only flows an average of three times a year. The sandy course and majestic river red gums which line the bed as well as the banks are all that most visitors see. But on the few occasions when it does flow, the mighty torrent is a grand spectacle which once seen is not easily forgotten. Locals crowd the causeways and bridges to watch the turbulent muddy waters carry the odd canoe or kayak downstream towards the Gap. While most flows subside quietly within a day, the Easter flow of 1988 flooded much of the town adjacent to the river.

Alice Springs is the only town of any size in the heart of Australia. As the lonely Stuart Highway forges northward, the monotony is broken only by refuelling stops for the car and its occupants. Relying on travellers, the tiny specks of Kulgera, Erldunda, Ti Tree and Barrow Creek consist of roadhouses and hotels, no more than pit stops for the car culture. But what a welcome respite from the endless strip of bitumen divided by an incessant broken white line. The challenge of overtaking a 50 metre long road train travelling at 100 kilometres an hour can be the afternoon's excitement, but there is something intriguing and relaxing about driving these vast distances through an unrelenting and unpopulated landscape. With no towns, traffic lights or cross-roads to focus one's attention, the mind is free to wander randomly as it chooses. Thoughts come and go, ideas expand and multiply, the occasional oncoming vehicle the only hint that other people do exist. But they quickly blur into the rear vision mirror as the road once again stretches towards the next horizon.

The nearest town to the Alice lies some 500 kilometres to the north. Tennant Creek owes its existence to the discovery of gold near the telegraph station by its telegraphist and linesman in 1925. These gold deposits have been worked ever since, but the town is also an important supply base for the many cattle stations of the Barkly Tableland. About 100 kilometres south, the Stuart Highway passes through a most unusual natural formation - the Devils Marbles. As its name implies, large rounded granite boulders lie scattered across a large field as if they were marbles of the giants. More astonishing still is that some are perched precariously atop others, seeming to defy the urge to just roll away.

Perhaps ironically, the only other town is situated in one of the most remote parts of the Centre. Nestled in sand dunes some 250 kilometres west of the Stuart Highway, lies the gleaming new town of Yulara, built in the early '80s to service the large numbers of tourists visiting Ayers Rock. These ancient sands, blown northwards for millions of years, now support the very latest architecture, in modern civilization's desire to see Nature's oldest creations.

European peoples' determination to populate the heart of Australia has undoubtedly succeeded. But considering the slow progress over the last 130 years, we should not think the next century will be dramatically different. Alice Springs will always be the main centre for people living or visiting this area, but the vast landscape surrounding the Alice will probably always be the domain of cattle stations, a few mines, and the growing hordes of people coming to visit the unspoilt environment which gives the heart of Australia its unique beauty.

The soft colours of sunset highlight a rainshower over the ranges surrounding Alice Springs.

The soft dawn twilight reveals Alice Springs and the Macdonnell Ranges.

After heavy rains, the Macdonnell Ranges can disappear into a blanket of low cloud.

The appropriately named Anzac Hill offers panoramic views of Alice Springs as well as spectacular skies.

Rising waters of the Todd River, in Alice Springs, turn many trees into islands.

The unusual sight of a flowing Todd River becomes more improbable with the addition of kayaks.

Numerous river red gums line the sandy bed of the Todd River.

With the causeway closed, spectators gather to watch the swift floodwaters of the Todd.

A sight familiar to highway travellers in the Centre, cattle-grids form a continuation of the fence lines across roads.

White lines and white posts relieve the monotony of this section of the Stuart Highway south of the Alice.

White ash indicates the position of a burnt out tree trunk, of which only the small branches are left, spread out on the surrounding sand.

Sun bleached bones, a wrinkled hide and a ball of partially digested grasses mark the final resting place of another highway casualty.

Corrugated iron modelled after the style of a bygone era reminds us of how Barrow Creek looked in the past.

Collapsed roofing iron and charred paintwork are grim indicators of the severity of a fire at the Aileron Hotel.

A delicately balanced granite boulder demonstrates the strange manner in which Nature has sculpted the Devils Marbles.

The late sun glows warmly on the spinifex and round, flaking boulders of the Devils Marbles.

Flocks of galahs are a common sight in Central Australia.

Zebra finches congregate in a noisy group, continuously chirruping away.

The glowing red eyes of the black-shouldered kite contrast vividly with its creamy white plumage.

A lone black swan glides across the waters of Ormiston Gorge.

AYERS ROCK AND THE OLGAS

ULURU - AYERS ROCK AND THE OLGAS

No matter how many times one sees Ayers Rock, each time seems as new as the time before, and as mysterious as the time before. No matter how often one has looked and contemplated this magnificent monolith, there is always something else to study, something new to notice. To feel familiar with its overwhelming presence, one would have to spend years living in its proximity, to experience its many changing moods, its dramatic displays of colour at the beginning and end of each day. And to be there when monsoonal downpours cloak the summit in a swirling mist, and see the colour change to a sombre brown, emphasizing the dark brooding weather.

This ageless desert landmark has been in its present form for perhaps 50 million years, during which time it has been sandblasted by the desert sands and eroded by torrents of water into an incredibly intricate shape, which is simply known as "The Rock". In this instance the word "rock" does nothing to convey the enormity of its size and the compelling nature of its presence. To the Aborigines who live there, the tourists who climb to the summit are known as Minga or small black ants. And indeed, as the lines of people move up and down the climb, they do look like little ants. While this comparison does some justice to the size, one can never compare the feeling of actually standing nearby one of its prominent features with the millions of photographs that have been taken. Very few images can capture the aura of the Rock, the compelling presence which draws people from all over the world to come and marvel at one of Nature's most famous works of art.

Some 30 kilometres to the west lies another of Nature's most extraordinary creations, the Olgas. Comprising 36 domes of varying sizes, this collection of steep-sided rocky protrusions looks like no other landscape on earth. Similar in some ways to Ayers Rock, the Olgas differ markedly in that while the Rock is a single monolith, the Olgas consist of many separate parts. It is believed that originally this formation was a single enormous dome several times the size of Ayers Rock.

The Aboriginal names for these marvellous features are of interest. The Olgas are known as Kata Tjuta or 'many heads', which seems very appropriate, while Ayers Rock is called Uluru, which is simply a name with no literal translation. Uluru is also the name given to the park which contains the two most outstanding features in the heart of Australia.

Rising abruptly to 348 metres above the surrounding plain, Ayers Rock can be seen from many kilometres away. Together with the Olgas, it totally dominates a landscape which otherwise consists mainly of sand dunes. With a circumference of 9.4 kilometres the base traces out a complex path as it cuts in and out to form several gorges. Created from sedimentary deposits 600 million years ago, Uluru and Kata Tjuta are part of an extensive bed of rock which stretches about 100 kilometres from east to west beneath the desert sands. These sediments came originally from the Musgrave and Mann Ranges, which at the time were enormous mountain ranges many thousands of metres high. For millions of years large deposits of sand, gravel and boulders were laid down on the slopes of these ancestral ranges, and were eventually compressed into the highly resistant sandstone which we know today. Subsequent erosion removed the less resistant rock strata, leaving behind the solitary shape of Uluru and multi-domed complex of Kata Tjuta. The addition of the sand dunes has been relatively recent.

While the Olgas' rock strata has been only slightly tilted, that of the Rock has been tilted as much as 85°, giving it a definite grain which runs towards the north-west. It is at the ends of these strata lines that the exotic erosion takes place, creating the numerous caves that occur all around. Many of these have fantastic shapes and contours, with distorted and extended fingers of rock hanging precariously from the roof or walls, at times looking for all the world like the inside bones or internal structure of the Rock. They are mysterious and haunting places which look like no other caves. Bats and birds utilize some of these caves, leaving behind odiferous piles of black droppings which stifle the still air inside.

The strata lines also give the Rock much of its character. Along the north-west side, the numerous scalloped channels descending steeply to the ground become gushing watercourses when it rains. After drying out, these channels retain dark algae growth lines, which give the false impression of water stains. These same strata channels continue right over the Rock, where they create deep gullies which must be traversed in the order to reach the summit.

Significantly higher than Uluru, the tallest dome of Kata Tjuta reaches 546 metres above the surrounding dunefield. In many ways more mysterious than Uluru, the domes crowd together over a few square kilometres of the desert. The steep sides of the main domes at the western end create narrow gorges through which walking is possible, but the awesome size of these gigantic rock walls makes one feel very humble indeed. From whichever way one views this ancient landscape, a different scene unfolds. Some of the domes are packed very closely together, some stand like solitary sentinels. Others have an elongated sloping shape, while nearby several may thrust upward with nearly vertical sides which gradually round off to cap the dome. Complex erosion patterns give individual domes a powerful presence, while some of the rock walls are stained with a variety of different coloured streaks. An air of mystery pervades the view, and a feeling of awe fills the mind as this ancient landscape reminds you of what the world may have looked like when dinosaurs walked the earth.

Both Ayers Rock and the Olgas are renowned for their incredible colour changes. Perhaps no single feature draws more people to view these monoliths than the spectacle of the rising or setting sun causing dramatic changes in their appearance and colour. Unhindered by trees or elevated horizons, the flat desert expanse allows the very last rays of the setting sun to transform the already warm colours of the rock into a blazing ember, which glows in the evening sky. With cloud effects, the changes are enhanced even more, the possibility of a rainbow or curtain of rain further exciting the imagination.

Perhaps no other event better dramatizes the appearance or further transforms the mood, than when one of the rare monsoonal downpours finds its way into the heart of Australia. To be there at such a time is a privilege. The spectacular images of the many waterfalls which descend from the mist-shrouded summit of Uluru remain fixed in one's memory forever. With the light softened by overcast skies, and the low cloud base dancing and swirling around the lightning scarred ridges, new shapes and forms reveal themselves. Tiny rivulets spill down steep shoulders while more substantial streams cascade down the beautifully sculptured contours which generally go unnoticed in the harsh midday sun. It is a truly rivetting experience.

More than any other natural feature, Uluru symbolizes the Australian landscape both at home and overseas. The vast expanse of desert which occupies such a large part of the Australian continent contains a great variety of unusual landscapes. To visit these remote places requires a long and sometimes arduous journey, but for the many people who have made the effort, there is nothing to compare with Uluru and Kata Tjuta, found in the heart of Australia.

Ayers Rock casts a long shadow as the late afternoon sun highlights the surrounding sand dunes.

The bright purple parakeelya flower dots the red sands surrounding Ayers Rock.

A pair of desert oak trees frame this late afternoon view of Ayers Rock, known also by the Aboriginal name of Uluru.

Scattered boulders around the base of the Rock hold sufficient moisture for these fig trees to grow.

The rising sun causes the Rock to glow brilliantly and at the same time highlights its layered nature.

An area of shady trees is flanked by the sheer walls of Kantju Gorge.

The timber-like grain of the descending stone ends abruptly in a cave large enough to accommodate a house.

Honey-combed erosion areas continue to shape the floor of the Kantju Gorge cave, while leaving behind a curved wall
supporting rocky remnants.

Unusual erosion patterns descend from the roof of the cave, while one of the fractured stones has been used as an art site.

As the sun descends the Rock glows with a continuous change in colour and intensity.

Early morning light reveals four prominent shoulders rising from the surrounding sandy plain.

Monsoonal weather shrouds the top of the Rock in a thickening cloud cover.

As the rain begins, waterfall courses become apparent all over the Rock.

A single stream of water flows out of the mist-shrouded top of Ayers Rock.

Numerous waterfalls cascade together down the steep sides of the Rock.

Several watercourses follow the twisted contours of the Rock to meet a fast flowing creek emanating from Mutitjulu.

A shoulder of the Rock disappears into the cloudbase which has obscured the entire top of Ayers Rock.

Swirling mist envelopes a rock valley from which a creek descends down a scalloped watercourse.

Low cloud and soft light reveal the gentle contours which go unnoticed under the normally harsh desert sun.

Fiery hues from the dawn twilight prompt the

Olgas to glow with an intense colour.

A rounded dome thrusts upwards, bearing the complex scars of eons of erosion.

Small waterholes form in the gorges between the major domes, washing down enough soil to sustain a few grasses and shrubs.

Early morning light warms a few of the domes of Kata Tjuta, an Aboriginal name meaning many heads.

The dramatic view from a ridge which saddles two domes of the Olgas, overlooking the Valley of the Winds.

OTHER BOOKS BY PETER JARVER

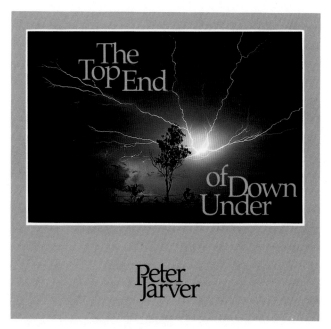

THE TOP END OF DOWN UNDER

KAKADU COUNTRY

LIMITED EDITION PHOTOGRAPHS

Limited edition photographs are offered to discerning people with an eye for the very best in quality and for their investment potential. All images from **Peter Jarver**'s three book titles are available as high quality Cibachrome photographs which are individually signed and numbered in an edition of 50. The special large format camera used in the making of these images guarantees that each one is exquisitely detailed, while possessing clarity and depth unmatched by other formats.

For further information write to:

Thunderhead Publishing,
GPO Box 2914, Darwin NT 0801.

FINE ART POSTERS

BLACK LIGHTNING 610mm x 726mm

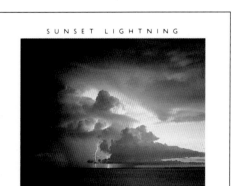

SUNSET LIGHTNING 610mm x 726mm

CLOUDBURST 610mm x 726mm

JIM JIM FALLS 610mm x 726mm

MISTY MORNING 610mm x 726mm

PANDANUS REFLECTION 610mm x 726mm

The fine art posters reproduced here are specially chosen images from the three book titles by Peter Jarver. They are printed on 200 gsm quality art paper to a size of 610 × 726 mm and are ideally suited for framing. They are available from galleries or by writing to:

Thunderhead Publishing,
GPO Box 2914, Darwin NT 0801.

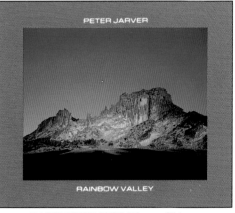

RAINBOW VALLEY 610mm x 726mm

VALLEY OF THE WINDS 610mm x 726mm

TECHNICAL DATA

COVER	Horseman FA 4x5, Schneider 90mm f8, polarizer	P.78 (TOP)	Rollei 6006 6x6cm, Distagon 40mm f4
P.9	Rollei 6006 6x6cm, Planar 80mm f2.8	P.78 (BOTTOM)	Rollei 6006 6x6cm, Planar 80mm f2.8
P.10	Horseman FA 4x5, Schneider 150mm f5.6, polarizer	P.79 (TOP)	Rollei 6006 6x6cm, Planar 80mm f2.8, 2 x converter
P.11	Horseman FA 4x5, Schneider 150mm f5.6, polarizer	P.79 (BOTTOM)	Rollei 6006 6x6cm, Distagon 40mm f4
P.12/13	Horseman FA 4x5, Schneider 150mm f5.6	P.80	Canon F1 35mm, Canon 20mm f2.8, polarizer
P.14	Horseman FA 4x5, Schneider 90mm f8	P.81	Canon F1 35mm, Canon 20mm f2.8, polarizer
P.15	Horseman FA 4x5, Nikkor 360mm ED f8	P.82	Canon F1 35mm, Canon 28mm f2
P.16	Horseman FA 4x5, Schneider 150mm f5.6, polarizer	P.83	Canon F1 35mm, Canon 20mm f2.8, polarizer
P.17	Horseman FA 4x5, Schneider 90mm f8, polarizer	P.84	Canon F1 35mm, Canon 28mm f2, polarizer
P.18	Horseman FA 4x5, Schneider 65mm f5.6	P.85	Canon F1 35mm, Canon 28mm f2
P.19	Horseman FA 4x5, Nikkor 360mm ED f8	P.86	Plaubel 69W 6x9cm, Schneider 47mm f5.6, polarizer
P.20	Horseman FA 4x5, Schneider 150mm f5.6, polarizer	P.87	Canon F1 35mm, Canon 28mm f2
P.21	Horseman FA 4x5, Schneider 90mm f8, polarizer	P.88 (TOP)	Canon F1 35mm, Canon 300mm f4L
P.22	Horseman FA 4x5, Nikkor 360mm ED f8, polarizer	P.88 (BOTTOM)	Canon F1 35mm, Canon 300mm f4L, 2 x converter
P.23	Horseman FA 4x5, Schneider 150mm f5.6, polarizer	P.89 (TOP)	Canon F1 35mm, Canon 300mm f4L, 2 x converter
P.24	Horseman FA 4x5, Nikkor 360mm ED f8, polarizer	P.89 (BOTTOM)	Canon F1 35mm, Canon 300mm f4L, 2 x converter
P.25	Horseman FA 4x5, Schneider 150mm f5.6, polarizer	P.93	Rollei 6006 6x6cm, Planar 80mm f2.8, polarizer
P.26	Horseman FA 4x5, Schneider 90mm f8	P.94	Horseman FA 4x5, Schneider 90mm f8, polarizer
P.27	Horseman FA 4x5, Schneider 150mm F5.6, 81A	P.95	Horseman FA 4x5, Schneider 90mm f8
P.28	Horseman FA 4x5, Schneider 65mm f5.6, polarizer	P.96	Horseman FA 4x5, Schneider 150mm f5.6, polarizer
P.29	Horseman FA 4x5, Nikkor 360mm ED f8, polarizer	P.97	Horseman FA 4x5, Nikkor 360mm f8
P.30	Plaubel 69W 6x9cm, Schneider 47mm f5.6, polarizer	P.98	Horseman FA 4x5, Schneider 90mm f8, polarizer
P.31	Plaubel 69W 6x9cm, Schneider 47mm f5.6, polarizer	P.99	Horseman FA 4x5, Nikkor 360mm f8, polarizer
P.32	Horseman FA 4x5, Nikkor 360mm ED f8, polarizer	P.100	Horseman FA 4x5, Schneider 90mm f8
P.33	Horseman FA 4x5, Nikkor 360mm ED f8, polarizer	P.101	Horseman 4x5, Schneider 90mm f8, 81A
P.34	Horseman FA 4x5, Schneider 150mm f5.6, polarizer	P.102 (TOP)	Horseman FA 4x5, Schneider 150mm f5.6
P.35	Horseman FA 4x5, Schneider 150mm f5.6	P.102 (BOTTOM)	Horseman FA 4x5, Schneider 150mm f5.6
P.36	Plaubel 69W 6x9cm, Schneider 47mm f5.6	P.103 (TOP)	Horseman FA 4x5, Schneider 150mm f5.6
P.37	Horseman FA 4x5, Nikkor 360mm ED f8	P.103 (BOTTOM)	Horseman FA 4x5, Schneider 150mm f5.6
P.38	Horseman FA 4.5, Schneider 90mm f8, 81A	P.104	Horseman FA 4x5, Schneider 150mm f5.6
P.39	Horseman FA 4x5, Schneider 90mm f8, polarizer	P.105	Horseman FA 4x5, Schneider 150mm f5.6
P.40	Horseman FA 4x5, Schneider 150mm f5.6, polarizer	P.106	Rollei 6006 6x6cm, Rolleigon 50mm f4
P.41	Horseman FA 4x5, Nikkor 360mm ED f8, polarizer	P.107	Rollei 6006 6x6cm, Planar 80mm f2.8, 2 x converter
P.42	Horseman FA 4x5, Schneider 65mm f5.6, polarizer	P.108	Horseman FA 4x5, Schneider 150mm f5.6
P.43	Horseman FA 4x5, Schneider 90mm f8, polarizer	P.109	Horseman FA 4x5, Nikkor 360mm f8
P.44	Horseman FA 4x5, Schneider 150mm f5.6	P.110/11	Horseman FA 4x5, Schneider 90mm f8
P.45	Horseman FA 4x5, Nikkor 360mm ED f8, polarizer	P.112	Canon F1 35mm, Canon 28mm f2, polarizer
P.46	Horseman FA 4x5, Nikkor 360mm ED f8, polarizer	P.113	Canon F1 35mm, Canon 20mm f2.8, polarizer
P.47	Horseman FA 4x5, Nikkor 360mm ED f8, polarizer	P.114	Horseman FA 4x5, Schneider 150mm f5.6
P.51	Plaubel 69W 6x9cm, Schneider 47mm f5.6, time exposure	P.115	Horseman FA 4x5, Schneider 65mm f5.6, polarizer
P.52	Horseman FA 4x5, Schneider 150mm f5.6, polarizer		
P.53	Horseman FA 4x5, Schneider 90mm, f8, polarizer		
P.54	Horseman FA 4x5, Schneider 150mm f5.6		
P.55	Horseman FA 4x5, Schneider 90mm f8		
P.56	Rollei 6006 6x6cm, Rolleigon 50mm f4, polarizer		
P.57	Rollei 6006 6x6cm, Rolleigon 50mm f4, polarizer		
P.58	Horseman FA 4x5, Schneider 90mm f8, polarizer		
P.59	Horseman Fa 4x5, Schneider 90mm f8, polarizer		
P.60/61	Plaubel 69W 6x9cm, Schneider 47mm f5.6		
P.62	Rollei 6006 6x6cm, Distagon 40mm f4, time exposure		
P.63	Horseman FA 4x5, Schneider 90mm f8		
P.64	Horseman FA 4x5, Schneider 90mm f8, polarizer		
P.65	Horseman FA 4x5, Schneider 90mm f8		
P.66	Horseman FA 4x5, Schneider 90mm f8, polarizer		
P.67	Horseman FA 4x5, Schneider 65mm f5.6, polarizer		
P.68	Horseman FA 4x5, Schneider 90mm f8, polarizer		
P.69	Horseman FA 4x5, Schneider 150mm f5.6, polarizer		
P.70	Horseman FA 4x5, Nikkor 360mm ED f8, polarizer		
P.71	Plaubel 69W 6x9cm, Schneider 47mm f5.6, polarizer		
P.75	Rollei 6006 6x6cm, Distagon 40mm f4		
P.76 (TOP)	Rollei 6006 6x6cm, Distagon 40mm f4		
P.76 (BOTTOM)	Rollei 6006 6x6cm, Distagon 40mm f4		
P.77	Canon F1 35mm, Canon 20mm f2.8		

Lens equivalents to 35mm format:

20mm	:	Schneider 65mm f5.6
		Schneider 47mm f5.6
24mm	:	Distagon 40mm f4
28mm	:	Schneider 90mm f8
		Rolleigon 50mm f4
50mm	:	Schneider 150mm f5.6
		Planar 80mm f2.8
115mm	:	Nikkor 360mm f8

The film of choice used in photographing this book was **FUJIFILM**

First published by Thunderhead Publishing 1990
GPO Box 2914 DARWIN NT 0801 Australia
Telephone (089) 81 6541. Facsimile (089) 41 0383

Designed by David Hughes Design
Melbourne, Australia
Printed by Dai Nippon
© Peter Jarver 1990

Jarver, Peter.
The Heart of Australia
ISBN 0 9589067 2 6

Acknowledgements:
Ken Visca of Hanimex for the Fujichrome film.
Staff and rangers of the Conservation Commission of the
Northern Territory.
Ian Trapnell for the Central Australian map.
Marilyn Venus for editing assistance.
Bureau of Meteorology, Darwin, for their advice on being in
the right place at the right time.
Landsat imagery provided by the Australian Centre for Remote
Sensing, Department of Administrative Services.
John Keegan for his companionship on the many trips.